In memory of Charlie Lee Davis, Mary G. Davis and Holline Brooks.

Dedicated to my wife, Pansy G. Davis, who has put up with me for forty-eight years.

Thanks to my readers: Mary, Nancy, Chuck, Dorothy, Boo and Shirley. Their reading gave me a reason to write. Thanks to my recent teachers, Gene Cahill and Robbie Britt, who encouraged me.

# Table of Contents

# Ode To A Coffee Urn

What filling is used in thee?
That always brings the crowd
Tempts and entices me
To sip your liquid aloud

Thou bubbling noise while brewing
A bean from some mountainside
Ground into a powder so soothing
We bow down without any pride

For we are an addicted lot
Drugged we return each day
Bowing before thy shiny pot
We worship with feet of clay

Producing such imbibing loves
With only a cup or two
Drawn together like two doves
Me and your happy brew

You are not a Grecian urn
But a ravished bride of delight
I wait in line for my turn
Even when you are out of sight

It is a wish to start my day
Not with a concoction mix
Not with condiments will I play
I will take a straight caffeine fix

And bow before you as a shrine
For you are the addictive urn
Better than Grecians anytime
The one for which I yearn

## Absolutes

Absolutes come in ones or twos
Not so many that I can't count
They are like singing the blues
Wisdom words from a font

To live by, I do not know
Maybe the overt ideology
Is just for outside show
Nothing for epistemology

There is an absolute I do know
Love is not a fleeting thing
Once it comes it will never go
It does not require a ring

Only the sight, touch or smell
Brings back the covered dish
Of the first time that I fell
Now turned into a covert wish

But it is a truth absolute
Love can not be any less
Starting from seed or root
Growth is the final test

Choosing it may be a game
Sometimes played by only one
If the choice is not the same
One unchosen, absolutely alone

# Abstract Art

If your lips do not seal
Against the white ceramic
Brown abstract art will form
On the front of your cup

Picasso it may not be
But this morning it was a tree
It had a full foliage top
Was it an upside down mop?

It could have been a cotton stalk
The top being in full bloom
One empty limb stuck out
Was it an ornament mount?

Maybe I'll make just a river
Holding the cup with a quiver
A simply wipe with the thumb
Or a lip with a muffin crumb

Can make the oddest things
With these brown coffee stains
Seems it is a dual purpose cup
While I drink my coffee up

# A Christmas Poem

Christmas is here I can tell
All the stores have lots to sell
Twinkling glowing, houses look grand
Some bright enough for planes to land

Bright lights bring good cheer it seems
Happiness comes through the beams
On some roofs a grinch does lurch
On his face a hateful smirk

From the lights he may draw his strength
To get you, he will go to any length
We must all have strength this time of year
Enjoy, laugh, and drink some beer

Have a mead and a nog for old times
Forget for a while all of your crimes
Good memories just feel the glow
Enjoy the day, let good cheer flow

Don't let any one spoil your day
'Tis the season for fun and play
Crank the voltage way up high
And pray the grinch will go on by

## A Cinquain

Comfort

The chair
Plump, fat and soft
Freely stands in the room
Positioned upright and waiting
For me

## A Tanka Poem

True Blue (Better old than new)

Soft wrinkled blue jeans
Grown white inside and outside
Worn thin at the Knee
Hanging by loops on a belt
Jeans are better old than new

# A Country and Western Song

You asked for my love
And I gave it to you
Now I am asking you
Why am I still blue?

Holding and loving you
Was so easy to do
Can't believe you'd say
That you and I are through

I thought we had a chance
For a real romance
Now you are saying goodbye
Without even a try

Refrain
So don't ask for my love anymore
I have had enough of your country lore

## A Funeral

Death is stillness
In time
Remembering others
Who were also still
With Flowers and Tears

Breaking the silence
With wet eyes
Family and friends
Who have their stillness
Yet to come

# A Ladder for Two

Why do we keep falling off the ladder?
For what's the purpose on a ladder?
Not afraid to risk a climb
Some ladder has a place for us

Must not fall too often, better to adjust
Stabilize, gain a strong foothold
Look up, look down, see what's around
Some ladder has a place for us

We two can be as one
Especially on a ladder
So hold on, be strong, be true
My ladder has a place for you

We will learn each time we fall
We can't defy the gravity law
So hold on, be strong, be true
My ladder has a place for you

## An Enticing Sound

The joy I heard
In your voice so soft
Was like a bird
Sending my spirits aloft

Like waves of light
Your voice was like sunshine
Brought you into my sight
A beauty for all time

For seeing with sound
Like a sixth sense
Brings joy all around
My perceptions condense

Into that ultimate feeling
Brought by your voice
Sends all other senses reeling
Siren, I have no choice

# Anger

From whence come angry words
Their source seems so very blurred
For they are often so quick to come
From such a small source they are begun

The blood pressure seems to rise
As anger will take me by surprise
Covering up what is underneath
Even volcanoes let their magna seep

It's emission from my discontent
Brain angry at a message sent
At both my enemies and my friends
I sometimes shoot darts and body pins

For the brain is triggered to go back
And bring forth the voice for attack
Trying to resolve that forgotten pain
The adrenaline flows once again

Why can't I mellow and forget
Those past hurts that linger yet
Lying underneath but not so low
Always waiting to strike a blow

Confusing wife, neighbors and friend
As I prove that I am nuts "agin"
Over reacting to such little things
Never accepting what real life brings

Some day the memories will go away
And I'll accept what's on my tray
And my anger will be no more
I won't need to balance the score

# A Tree Laments About Loss of Limbs

Isabel a weapon of mass destruction
Came flying through our town
It whirled with quite some suction
And tried to blow me down

My trunk was not really harmed
But it blew two limbs askew
My owner became quite alarmed
And I was a bit shaken too

A call was made for a surgeon
And he came immediately
I did not like the curmudgeon
He was very rough with me

He tried a bandage and a prop
He held my arms up with a crane
But one arm fell kerplop
And I began to feel some pain

Then George, my owner, spoke
We had better use the old chain saw
These limbs are really broke
The bone saw cuts left me raw

Now all of the surgery is done
I have two scars of white
It wasn't a lot of fun
But I seem to be all right

# A Whale

A whale with a table
Sitting on its back
Now out of the water
As a coffee cup rack

Sculptured with glass cover
As our piece of the sea
Now sits on the pedestal
Between my wife and me

And each time we look
We know where we found
That humpback a blowing
In the Ketchikan sound

One memory in bronze
Forever it will last
For it holds together
A bit of our past

All memories can't be
Converted to stone
But our brain synapses
Carries others along

## Back When

Back when I didn't have anything girls wanted
I had acne, but no car
I had need, but no money
I had smarts, but no education

Back when I didn't have What the girls wanted?
Back when virginity sold
I couldn't buy an option
Who was the highest bidder?

I had no dough
I had no wheels
Without these things
I couldn't make deals

Those were the days
The girls were slim and trim
I just wanted one of them
But that was way back when

I was the one who went in waiting
Back when I didn't have anything
But the out of sight future and
Girls who would not wait

Now
I have a car
I have an education
I have money

No virgins my age

Now that I have
What the girls want
I get that old feeling

When I take Viagra
Or swallow a Levetra
Use lasting Cialis
What do girls really want?

## Bantu Writings

The water tower above the lake
A tree on a grassy knoll

Hovering hawk over a mouse in the field
A gun ship over an immigrant in the desert

Lily pads
Water covers

Tremoring hands
Cups of Jell-O

Going into Debt
Selling your soul

A full bucket
Life overflowing

## Chandelier

Of all the things that I'd be
I'd be a bulb in your chandelier
Up high for everyone to see
Shining for whom I care

I might not be the brightest
And I would not be alone
But I would not contest
For that would be my home

We would be together
And I would feel at rest
For it would be a feather
I would feel I was the best

Of all the chandliers I've seen
You are the most elegant
So be my lighting queen
I'll be your supplicant

# Cloud Making

Clouds go in and out
Like high jumping trout
I watched a cloud go away
Like it was hide and seek play

Turning this way and that
Sometimes skinny, sometimes fat
Now it's here, now it's gone
Losing shape, what is wrong?

The cloud maker must have fun
Playing with his cloud making gun
Painting here and painting there
Always leaving some splotch bare

It must be some magic trick
Getting water molecules so thick
They can be seen with the naked eye
As large white figures in the sky

The cloud maker must be asleep
Leaving molecules in a heap
But the out line is still there
Even looks like wispy hair

It fell as rain from the skies
And disappeared from my eyes
Now on the ground the cloud is laid
I wish the cloud maker could have stayed

# Color Chart

With culture come a lot of colors
More than a rainbow can give
Red is no longer red
And green is no longer green
But loneliness is still gray

Colors are spun just like politics
You can be celery green
Buttercup replaces yellow
Strawberry replaces red
But cold is still purple

French navy is not ships
Macaroni and cheese is not food
Razzmatazz is not for fun
And cornflower is not on corn
But hunger is a color that you cannot hide

Colors by the numbers
Can fill a canvas white
Mixtures blend so easily
Cultures can't seem to play the game
But Terrorism is still black and white

A bomb has no color
It brings see-through tears
Ethnic cleansing brings the color red
Mixing with the chocolate dust
Producing the color, revenge

It puts mankind on a regressive path
Thousands of colors will be erased
And we will go back to the garden
Where red apples are the fruit
And all civilized colors will be gone

# Cotton Picking

The green field turns white
It is a time for picking
Remove the fiber from each shell
Handfuls into the canvas sack

Pulled upon the ground
Between the rows of green and white
Start with the early light
Bent over until the sun goes down

Pulling the sack behind
Fill and pack it down
Take a rest in the sun
Sitting on a cotton filled bag

The rows seem to never end
Except when conversation fills in
Maybe a joke or a memoir
From early days gone by

Exaggeration from the past
Of pounds that filled each sack
Numbers get lost and transposed
Picking lies are never quite exposed

The pickers turn the rows to green
Wagons take the white away
And frost will paint stalks brown
When pickers go back to town

But they will come again
For each fall the field turns white
Stories and sacks will spring forth
And backs will be sore once more

# Crack in the Record

We were to be the replete song
But you put a crack in my record
Like a bolt from the sky
We were separated, you and I

My record broke axis to edge
When you shoved me off the ledge
Registered as a perpetual defect
Grinds and plays like an old reject

But the record still has to play
Until that crack is fixed some day
Life long grooves will be aberrant
And that crack will cripple my chant

# Cry for Help

Why do I cry out to you?
After all these years are through
I should know the answer by now
This relationship just won't plow

But still I linger with care
Hoping some day you'll be there
Standing as I remember in green
I walked away with tears unseen

From words I could not believe
Knowing that other words did deceive
Those that expressed undying love
Were not sworn by God above

That was a real heart tattoo
Ending love between me and you
What we had came to an end?
I have a love I can not defend

Except I know it still exists
Though all the turns and twists
Lingering on for all these years
Encapsulated with all my fears

Like a broken record it plays
The nights are worse than days
Fantasying is all I have left
And it's all kept upon the shelf

# Déjà vu

Déjà vu is what it is called
Or is it just being enthralled
Dreams of you so oft return
Awake, I am prone to yearn

Taking a walk is not safe
For in my brain you'll take a place
And no matter how I try
Dreams of you keep coming by

Sleeping brings no respite
I can't get you out of sight
Dreams come again, déjà vu
Asleep, now as always it is you

# Departing Pastor

Thanks for being my friend
As well as my pastor
Thanks for being there
When I needed you most
It was not on Sunday
But you were there anyway
Thanks for reasoning with me
When my thoughts were unreasonable
Thanks for coming into my depression
And leading me up the ladder
Thanks for not judging my sins
But always offering to help me
My pastor may change
But a friend like you is forever

# Dreams That Reoccur

What kind of dream is this?
Never a night will it miss?
Always searching for a place
It seems in a hurried pace

I have a schedule I must make
Not knowing the route to take
It is a place to be today
But I have again lost my way

Often it is some book I have lost
Dreams full of old roads I've crossed
Looking for the car I parked
Why wasn't the position marked?

Sometimes I am late for class
I do not even have a pass
After missing the whole semester
Another college class disaster

Then I am looking for my room
It is urgent I must find it soon
Could it be on this floor?
No, I will check some more

Why won't the elevator stop?
My kidneys are about to pop
Where is that room of rest?
After all I am a hotel guest

My yearning dreams go on and on
They seem to have a familiar tone
Bringing me back each night for more
One of these times I am gonna score

# Embarrassment

Red moves up to the top
Like a thermometer
When a pretty girl looks at me
I feel out of place

Wanting to be some place else
But not really
Just wanting to feel more comfortable
With what I see

I say a word like
"Hello"
And she responds
"Hello"

The red gets darker as
I stumble to say
"It is a nice day"
Meaning do you want to play

My tongue freezes
And I look down
I know by then
She thinks I am a clown

I can't look up
She is looking at me
But what can I say
"Read any good books lately?"

"Seen any scary movies?"
All dumb things to say

I look up
She is smiling

I think she is laughing
At me?
Is my fly open?
"Shaving cream behind my ears?"

She smiles and says, "My name is Priscilla"
What is yours?"
And what do you do?"
The color is fading

# Empty Shell

This morning I felt empty
Yet I have abundance by any measure
My thoughts have no substance
Words are like empty shells
The embryo has escaped

# Enter You into My Thoughts

If I failed to go with you
Will this be the last without question?
For the future to come will be a horrid time
With you touching and seeing the earth
With someone else

Before you failed to enter, without care.
What could I do?
Of care, of passion and of virtue—you were disguised.
Like an herb leaf in a fossil.
I was not allowed to enter

I live now, in solitude, in a chamber
You, you come again and again, enlarged
While I am vague, diminished
And forlorn, longing for fruit
Like a grape you once gave me

Enchantment with you still rules
Only you, I can walk with
This hour is ill, unrest rules
Venting vagueness, I toil, I sway
I hope you respond

It is this hour or never
For the past encloses, enslaves
A martyr for all of time
Enter you, enter you without ceasing
Your vine entangles me into your disguise

# Enticing Catalog Colors

Whisper to me with whisper pink
The color makes the woman
That is what the catalog said
With the pushup poinsettia red

Vintage yellow is not so old
Covering the curvaceous form
Of a Victoria Secret moll
In her enticing baby doll

The aqua brings to life
Both young and old alike
The color worn as a panty
Will enhance an exquisite fanny

Cornfields do come to mind
In that cornflower blouse
Cut low in front and back
Would enhance any old flour sack

All of these colors
For two piece bathing suits
Just send me one of each
And we will all go to the beach

# Free Mind

When I have a free mind
I think only of you
When I have a free mind
That is all I do

The baggage goes away
And today is all for living
The baggage goes away
Could you be forgiving?

I see the possibilities of life
And all the worlds treasures
I see the possibilities of life
And with you, what a pleasure!

# Front Porch

The front porch is a place to stand
With your girlfriend out of sight
Of her parents in the house
Only the nosey neighbors can see

That is where you start holding hands
That is where I felt so grand
When she put her arms around me
Brought a rush, I could hardly see

We started our love for each other
Saying there would never be another
We sat in the swing making plans
While we were holding hands

That is where we said goodbye
I can not believe our love was a lie
We went our separate ways
An the porch weathered empty

The swing is lonely in the breeze
No new plans are being made
The chains are covered with rust
Old boards are covered with dust

But I still remember the life started there
The life I couldn't hold
My love is still standing
Peeled and warped like the porch

The front porch is only a memory
But the times spent are still real
They will always be a part of me
I will go back every chance I get

# Furtive Eyes

The furtive eyes of men
From under the baseball caps
Look on high chested girls
Watch hips in motion
Tapered from slim waists

Never look at ankles
Covered with farmer brogans
Or calves covered with jeans.
Until the legs and ankles glide in nylon
The furtive looks will stay
Thigh level or higher

# History

History has lost its power
Replaced by up-close TV news
We watch it by the hour
And don't give the past its due

Why can't we recall the pain?
And what war does to me and you
Why do we have to see it again?
It makes another day to rue

Yes, history has lost its power
We make the same mistakes
What good are a grave and a flower?
When replaced by propaganda fakes

Many the lessons are not learned
Prevented by politics and corporate power
Can't believe we are not concerned
We have all been forced to cower

We are not using our history at all
Follow lock step the latest spin
And again some have to fall
Our history is flowing thin

Must it always gush in vain?
We will not listen to the truth
It seems we have all gone insane
And turned the politicians loose

# I Was Surprised

She took me by the hand
And led me to her bedroom
The sheets were turned down
I was surprised

She wore only a shirt
I unbuttoned the shirt
Revealing a red bra and panties
I was surprised

She help me remove my clothes
She pulled me to the bed
I followed her all the way
I was surprised, was I ever surprised?

# Love and Candles

Marriage
Two into one
Come together in love
Like two candles on life's table
Now one

# Couplets

Weddings fill Churches
Tears fill women's eyes

Wedding dress contrast
Necks covered, shoulders bare

Weddings and funerals
Pull families together

Marriage is the end
Or is it the beginning?

Search for a mate
Who is the hunted?

Survival of the fittest
Politicians supported by lobbyists

Searching for the truth
Don't watch television

A friend died yesterday
Now I am less

Support structure falling
Good friends are dying

It was delicious, delightful
It was damn good

## Love it or Leave it

Are you a flag burner?
Stand up and be counted
You cannot move out
If you do not leave the station

Death is here and there
Bring them on
You can't go home again
After you step on the banana peel

It is a slippery slope
If you do not like Mom's apple pie
Love it or leave it
Is pie or death the only choice?

Will you go to the end of the earth?
For your flag and your pie
Patriotism is in the eye of the beholder
We are beholden

But not through political eyes
For reality will be distorted
Even the red white and blue
Are different from the left and right

Are you one of the bad guys?
Bring them on
Right is might
I must go on alone

I cannot see the forest
There are too many trees
But I have my flag
He gave his life

And they gave me a flag
There were no strings
At least that is what I thought
I did not have any questions

# Memories

When bad memories go away
And good memories are here to stay
My mind goes searching
And finds you every time

There is that special place
Obscured except sometimes
My brain only entertains
Thoughts of you

I ask myself why
This memory phenomenon
Keeps filling my brain
Excluding all others

There is no answer
Words are not a part
Except to express
The longing I feel

When all else
Becomes a void
And my thinking
Turns only to you

# Nude Singing (A Bar Fancy)

And thus she sang
All naked as she sat
We boys got quite a bang
When she removed her hat

Her tresses fell to the floor
And her beauty shown through
We were all yelling for more
When a fellow came out of the blue

He yelled, "Get back on the horse"
For you are the Godiva lady
We were all filled with remorse
He took away the lady, so shady

But we run out to see
The horse she was going to ride
Some of us climbed a tree
She looked even better outside

Brightly shined the sun
And her tresses started flowing
As the horse began to run
Her nakedness was really showing

She sang in time with the gallop
The song was so beautiful
Some have said she was a trollop
I think she was just being dutiful

Our glasses rang with a clang
For we all toasted "that"
A lady riding away who sang
Still naked as she sat

# Ode to Jimmy Carter

I read the poems of Jimmy
They took me back
Through space and time
Back to a boyhood, mine

On a farm
Raising corn and cotton
And broomcorn for brooms
All raised in Oklahoma

Like the corn
I was ripe to leave
Feeding around the world
Finding a better purpose

Like the cotton
I was certain
I could weave
A beautiful tapestry

Like the broom
I keep on sweeping
And the changes sought
Will be in genes combined

# Paths

Our paths are determined it seems
By our sires and our childhood dreams
Even though the path be bent and dark
We keep trying to make our mark

Past failures spur us on
Trying to learn as we go along
But we return to the same old path
Makes an old man want to laugh

# Prepared

I was prepared for my heart to stop
I looked for you all over the shop
I searched for you up and down
Alas you were not to be found

In some ways it was quite a relief
For the sight brings both joy and grief
But I would have taken any pain
Just to see your beauty once again

My heart is back to a normal pace
For there was no sight to start the race
For only you can stop and start
The rapid palpitation of my heart

# Rag Top Sonnet

Seems nothing can replace the rag top car
For it still provides the ultimate ride
Blondes, redheads and brunettes from near and far
All will rush to be sitting by your side
The sky opens and the wind rushes by
The road is only a place for the wheels
For you see the road and she sees the sky
Only the wind knows how she really feels

Still the rag top is man's best device
For to lure a woman to take a ride
And start the courting to further entice
A woman of choice to stay by his side
Maybe when your rag top is on the blocks
And you have lost your charm and curly locks
She won't be looking for another rag top

# Sharing-Thoughts
## (After reading Carter's Poems)

The sharing of a beginning
And the growing
Was more than reading?
But a sharing in writing
Of times past
Not forgotten
Always on the warmer
Ready to serve, feel, taste,
Smell and hear
The sound from the past
Like resonance was mine
Started by a cool breeze
From Georgia

# Six Line Poem

Blue water, blue sky and her green eyes
She was the prettiest girl in the country town
When the summer brought a skin of brown
I wish I could go back in place and time
I want to see her and my friend Roy
Next year, I may go back to that country town

# Skirts

Skirts have lost their power
To fill my fanciful dreams
Those I use to watch by the hour
Now are pants, shorts and jeans

Was it the power of the skirt?
Or just my juvenile eyes?
That brought my mind to flirt
And produce those adoring sighs

I was always pleasantly surprised
With those long stems pushing hems
Which heels and hose emphasized?
Legs, I have seen some gems

I use to pray for a breeze
To blow those skirts up high
So I could see some knees
In loose skirts passing by

I still see skirts on the rack
Maybe their power is not all lost
I plan to live until they come back
Though this stone is gathering moss

# Talking to Myself

A greeting was not
What I had in mind
Just talking quite a lot
About the good old time

Did not say "Hello self"
It did not seem necessary
We are on the same shelf
And talking makes me dreary

You were such a dummy
To let that good time pass
It was not so funny
Why didn't you ask?

Why did I not do that?
Where am I now going?
The road is no longer flat
For this memory I'm towing

Can I live with myself?
Can I live without her?
How much time is left?
Now she is just a blur

Why not speak out loud?
Ask for forgiveness again
Don't lose her in the crowd
She must think I am insane

But I will have to continue

Even though she is gone
I must have more sinew
Can I ever right that wrong

# The Lady Said

She told me about my sister
Gone for thirty years or more
Still a freshened memory
I could not speak

The lady said, "Your sister
Was a kind person to me
She was so helpful
When I lost my Mother"

Back the memories flew
Into childhood pictures
When we played together
When we worked together

When we fought
Over toys
Over teasing
Over nothing

We had some, some memories
Cooking supper for our Mom
Hoeing the cotton and corn
Cutting and carrying wood

We got wet together
Walking to catch the yellow school bus
We shared a kerosene lamp
Getting our homework

Later times spent together

Her family and mine
We did not have to speak
We talked with our eyes

No other person
Gave me such understanding
Not a judgmental voice
Only a directional look

I learned over again
That I need her so much
When the lady said,
"Your sister was so kind"

# Transposing Numbers

Why did my sister die at thirty-nine?
It seemed too early in her time
She had not written her poems
She had not told her stories
There was some molding left to do
With her young children—two

I had not shared with her
My innermost feelings
Nor made my apologies
Hadn't told her about my love
Does she know of my loneliness?
Without her - - -

God, why not ninety-three
Instead of thirty-nine
Was it your plan?
Or did you transpose the numbers

# Trapped on a Bus

Forty-six people trapped on a bus
The lack of space makes us wanna cuss
Through the mountains, plains, and hills
Seeing wild animals our only thrills
Getting on and off the bus
Takes quite awhile for all of us
Seems we are getting slower every day
Riding this bus is no longer play
We will all have letters to write
To our travel agent we'd like to fight
About getting us up to leave at seven
The luggage didn't get loaded till eleven
The earlier we leave the quicker we'll see
That bald eagle sitting in a tree
And can you believe the moose we saw
Made us keep our cameras ready to draw
We traveled desert and farms of wheat
Stopped in Diners for a bite to eat
Back on the bus for a sit up nap
Wishing my head in someone's lap
Because the head falls forward and to the side
This was no first class airplane ride
But it was all over; we got to Salt Lake
A tour bus, never again, will I take

# Unfinished Memory

Searching, I came up blank
Visions not yet complete
Sent me looking with askance
Into my memory seat

Titles without pictures
The missing were of you
Things not happened
That I really wanted to

Some memories I want
Keep on evading me
They have not transpired
Into a full picture to see

Why this searching desire?
Something has slipped by me
Hidden from my view
The shell is always empty

I now know
What I want it to be
If it is ever finished
There is a role for you and me

Is it going to happen?
Will it come some day?
The worn out title will be
The memory that got away

# Urgent Travel

Where must I go?
And why so fast
I had rather travel slow
This journey I want to last

A journey not in time or space
I want so much to visit
The memory of you in lace
First class I wouldn't miss it

I won't go by train or car
What on earth should I pack?
I really want be going far
Who knows when I'll be back?

Travel memories are ill defined
The mind will jump the track
The travel cannot be timed
When memory is on the rack

The journey will be dangerous
As I travel through the maze
To see you, Mountain climb I must
I will strive for just a gaze

Seeing your beauty one more time
Is a journey often made
In this feeble brain of mine
For your memory does not fade

# When Time Feels Too Far Gone

When time feels too far a way
I know the past is slipping by
Still you are in that time to stay
Only the vision seems to lie

For you are still under the tree
Sunlight showing on your skin
With green eyes looking at me
I wish I were there again

For I would not go on past
I would run and grab your hand
I would speak words so fast
"You are the prettiest in the land"

Time keeps drifting round and round
I stand still, waiting it seems
Knowing that you can not be found
But you are vivid in my dreams

For time has moved too far gone
Since you walked out and away
I moved inside and stayed alone
In order to make it through the day